Disappearing Ontario

Disappearing Ontario

To Elise
with best wishes

Ron Brown

Polar Bear Press, Toronto

Polar Bear Press

distributed by:
North 49 Books
35 Prince Andrew Place
Toronto, Ontario M3C 2H2
416 449-4000

Canadian Cataloguing in Publication Data

Brown, Ron 1945-
Disappearing Ontario: images from our vanishing countryside

Includes index.
ISBN 1-896757-12-X

1. Historic sites – Ontario. 2. Historic sites – Ontario – Pictorial works. 3. Historic buildings – Ontario. 4. Historic buildings – Ontario – Pictorial works I. Title

FC3061.B755 1999 971.3 C99-932140-4
F1058.B755 1999

Printed in Canada

99 00 10 9 8 7 6 5 4 3 2 1

Table of Contents

Introduction

There was once a time when Ontario could boast of its countryside. Cattle munched happily on rolling pastures, grain waved golden in the late summer sun as far as the wood lot at the back of the farm. Handsome 19th century farm houses and rugged wooden barns fit comfortably in a landscape of field, woods, and tree-lined farm lanes.

It was a landscape that told the story of an evolution from forest to farm. But by the end of the millemium all that had changed. Throughout the 1990s, those responsible for the stewardship of the land increasingly put profit first. Speculators gobbled up massive amounts of land to cover it over with an endless vista of dreary look-alike houses. Strip malls lined the country roads, stretching endlessly, or so it seemed.

Ontario's politicians seem to be less aware of this environmental degradation, or simply don't care. The rise to power of the Mike Harris government during the late 1990s brought with it the abrogation of political involvement in all aspects of Ontario's natural and built heritage. Staff responsible for the protection of the environment and natural resources were fired by the thousands. Policies that protected farmland, and kept urban sprawl at bay, were abandoned. Conservation authorities, arguably the most effective single agency in saving old mills and heritage buildings (Toronto's popular Black Creek Pioneer Village was the result of such an initiative) were stripped of their mandate and their funding for such efforts by the same government.

But despite the eroding of political will, many success stories can be found: mills have been bought and restored by local historical societies, or by private individuals, bridges have been preserved as pedestrian walkways, old farm homes and log cabins proudly cared for.

This volume is not a lament for Ontario's vanishing country icons, but a celebration of them. While it may not be possible to save or preserve the landscape that once made this province a place of beauty, or to keep every aging mill or barn in its place, it is possible to preserve their legacy. I hope the images on the following pages contribute in some small way to that effort.

Ron Brown
September 1999

Grist mills

They numbered in the thousands, standing guard over Ontario's many rushing rivers and babbling brooks. They have been the subject of paintings from as early as the 1820s to the present, and honoured in song, poetry and prose. They are, of course, the old mill.

When Ontario's earliest pioneer settlers began to hack into the dark, brooding forests, they had no mills to grind their grain. To make flour for bread, farm women would pulverize the wheat by hand, a long and laborious chore. Once a horse was acquired, it could be used to power a treadmill until the earliest windmills began to intrude into the pioneer landscape.

In the 1790s Ontario's earliest grist mills began to appear. Because many of the earliest Loyalist landings were located along the lakes and in the protected coves, the first mills tended to appear at the nearest water power site upstream from the harbour. Toronto's "old mill" sits on the site of one such first mill, the Backus mill, another is a short distance upstream from Port Rowan. Built in 1797, the Backus mill is Ontario's oldest mill, having survived the American invasion of 1813 when all the other Lake Erie mills were burned. With its water wheel creaking, it grinds grain by water power to this day.

With the development of export markets in Britain between 1815 and 1845, and with the United States between 1854 and 1866, Ontario's mills quickly multiplied in number. By the 1830s there were 600 and by the 1880s, more than 1000.

As the century progressed, milling technology changed. While the earliest mills used creaking water wheels to convert water flow into power, by the mid-1800s turbines were in almost universal use. The traditional mill stones, most of them imported from France, were replaced by more efficient rollers. As the milling industry grew and flourished, flour mills began to replace the grist mills. (Grist mills specialized in custom grinding grain for individual farmers, the miller keeping a portion in return, while flour mills purchased the grain outright, grinding it into flour for export.)

Rivers with steady flows and steep profiles tended to have

The skeletal shell and the dry flume tell the fate of the former mill in Parham. Located near the fringe of the rugged Canadian Shield north of Kingston, the village's milling days were limited by the poor nature of much of the area's soil.

the most mills. The Humber and Credit contained as many as 80. Even the smaller Don at one point could count 18. On the other hand, sluggish rivers like the Thames contained few.

The demise of Ontario's mills began near the close of the century. With the opening of the prairies in the 1880s and 90s, western wheat replaced Ontario wheat and dairying became the mainstay of most southern Ontario farmers. The clearing of forests had a devastating effect on water tables, lowering it especially in the summer to the point where many smaller streams could no longer provide a reliable water power supply. The heyday of the Ontario grist mill was ending with the century.

Mills sat silent and the streams rushed by unimpeded. Floods roared down the streams carrying away mill dams, mills and sometimes entire mill towns. As a conservation measure, reservoirs were built to contain spring runoff, flooding many mill sites. Belatedly, the historical appreciation of Ontario's old mills began to take shape even after early mills had long vanished. Ontario's conservation authorities have perhaps been the most active of mill preservationists despite the efforts of the Ontario government to deprive them of their mandate to preserve history. In conservation areas such as the Backus conservation area, and the Bruce's Mill conservation area, in pioneer villages such as Toronto's long standing Black Creek, Lang near Peterborough and Doon Pioneer Crossroads near Waterloo, at museums, such as Otterville, and Morningstar Mills, and even in many private hands such as in Tyrone, history lives, and the mills grind on.

This fine stone mill was built by John Ferguson in 1857 and operated as a grist mill until 1940. Now a stone residence it is located on the Rocky Saugeen River near Durham.

This unadorned mill in Chesley, Ontario, still operates on water power, yet lies on the back streets of the village, little celebrated, still fulfilling its ancient role.

The Coldwater mill, one of Ontario's most historic, was established in 1833 by the government for the use of the local Ojibway band.

Although its milling days are done, the Birge mills is privately owned, and is one of the many handsome stone mills built throughout Wellington County, a region widely known for its Scottish stone heritage.

The hard work of the South Norwich Historical Society led to the preservation of Otterville's old Treffry mill in a community park. The mill was built in 1807 and was one of the longest in Ontario to function on water power. Otterville's station, too, has been saved and rests now on the nearby grounds of the local museum.

A community landmark since the 1840s, the Ball mill in Baltimore, north of Cobourg, has been saved. Built in 1834, it was operated by members of the Ball family until 1952 when operations ceased. Work on its preservation have continued sporadically since 1971.

The historic Mountain Mills at the Decew Power plant in St. Catharines is now a popular local museum. It was built by Robert Chappel in 1872 and rebuilt by Wilson Morningstar following a fire in 1884. It has since been known as the Morningstar Mills.

The 1842 grist mill in the living pioneer village of Tyrone, which also contains a traditional general store and blacksmith shop, has added a water power sawmill, and recently resumed grinding grain, also by water power. Cider is made on site using local apples.

Another view of the grist mill in Tyrone.

The stone grist mill at Allans Mills near Perth sat empty for many years before being converted to a house. Erected by William Allan, the mill was the focus for a community which also contained sawmills, a blacksmith, a wagon maker and a general store. Allan's stone house also survives.

One of Ontario's most photographed mills is the historic grist mill, also now a house, in the ghost town of Bedford Mills, north of Kingston. It dates from 1848 when the town was the busy milling empire of Benjamin Tett who also operated four sawmills nearby.

The Moira River rushes past the ruins of the Latta mill north of Belleville, one of forty mills on this fast-flowing river. Latta itself contained three sawmills as well as the grist mill.

James Stark built this imposing structure in Paisley in 1884 incorporating a new technique for rolling rather than grinding grain. The mill operated primarily as a flour mill before becoming a feed mill in later life.

The ruined walls of the Doon mill have been stabilized and preserved near Kitchener. When constructed in 1834 as the Ferrie mill, it was believed to have been the largest grist mill west of Montreal.

This old grist mill at Maple Hill near Hanover is gone now, and the village has been replaced with rural sprawl. Its board and batten construction was typical of many of the vanished mills in this region.

The stone mill at Martintown, near Cornwall, sits picturesquely on the banks of the Raisin River in the centre of the village. It was built by Alexander McMartin in 1846. This historic village retains many homes and stores from its early days with few modern intrusions.

Another eastern Ontario stone beauty, the Glen Tay grist mill on the Tay River is believed to have been built as early as 1820. Its days as a mill ended in 1918 and it stood vacant for over three decades before a brief revival as a vermiculite processing plant.

John Deagle's grist mill by the waterfall on the Credit River, which gave the name Cataract to the nearby village, was converted to a power plant around the turn of the century and provided electrical power as far away as Orangeville. Today it is a ruin situated along the Bruce Trail within the Forks of the Credit Provincial Park.

The former mill in Arden, now converted to a house, fits in well with this forgotten back-water community. Located south of Highway 7 near Sharbot Lake, Arden's streets remain lined with many of the old stores and hotels which once made it a thriving town. Most of these buildings, however, now sit empty.

Farm houses

Smoke wafts upward through the dark forest. Nestled in a small clearing, a simple log shanty shields a pioneer family from the sun and the rain. However, the log lean-to lets in everything else, the heat, the cold and the incessant black flies and mosquitoes. For their first season, the new arrivals could count on little else. These simple shelters may have measured only three metres by four, with no separate rooms, with tables and chairs made of crude planks, and only a hearth for heat and cooking.

By the next season, more logs were cut, and a larger log cabin built. Chinked with clay or moss, they were warmer, and may have even included a separate bedroom for the family parents. This usually lasted until the farm began to earn income, and planks could be had from a nearby sawmill to build a still more elaborate frame dwelling.

But it may not have been until the second or third generation that a farm home which could be called truly comfortable was placed on the land. Bricks were often used by then, or stone. Many farm homes from this phase still survive, and give the farm landscape the features that characterize it today.

The same may not be said for the first or second phase homes. The shanty, especially, has long left the farmscape. Here and there, perhaps sheltering a few foul, or a collection of farm tools, an original shanty may linger. In a few regions, the second phase log cabin may still stand. These are usually in those areas which were settled later, and where farm prosperity evaded the struggling farmers, denying them the opportunity to upgrade their homes. The more rugged reaches of the Ottawa Valley have a heavy concentration of log cabins, as do many of the back roads of Muskoka, Parry Sound and Hastings.

Many of the frame homes, too, have been removed, being expensive to insulate and subject to rot or warping. Often in their place are modern, sprawling ranch-style country estates.

The most common style of farm home was known as the storey-and-a-half home. These consisted of a full ground floor, but the second floor had a sloped roof. From 1807 to

1857 this style of home enjoyed a lower tax rate than did those with two full storeys. During this period nearly every farm home was constructed to this pattern. To gain more space some second floor rooves were built with a steeper pitch or dormers were added.

But during the later years of the 19th century many changes swept the farm community. The switch from wheat farming to dairying brought a new prosperity to the Ontario countryside. Finally farm families could build larger and more comfortable housing. A greater range of house patterns began to circulate, often published in farm magazines, such as Canada Farmer. Farming changed from being a subsistence or family operation to a commercial enterprise. The forms of architecture found in the towns and cities began to make their way into the countryside, with neo-classical, Victorian and Italianate homes suddenly appearing beside the old barns.

Ironically, the ethnic roots of the farm family were more likely to be reflected in barn style rather than in home styles, except for the traditionally French Canadian houses found along the lower Ottawa River. While the house styles were more likely provided in magazines, or dictated by local building contractors, the barns were left up to the farmers and here the varying styles reflected the roots of the settlers themselves. While many of these more solid farm homes still survive, others are being replaced by modern houses, better insulated, and more suited to today's needs for larger bedrooms and bathrooms and air conditioning.

The past 20 years has seen the arrival of wasteful rural sprawl. Across Ontario, excessive land severances, and massive subdivisions of monster estate homes have all diminished Ontario's countryside appearance. Whether they have been replaced or overwhelmed, the farm homes are yet another victim.

House and barn stand empty, gaunt reminders of dreams that went wrong, and families forced to abandon their hopes. Although such cases are found throughout Ontario, this example sits in a relatively prosperous farming area between the villages of Hastings and Stirling north of Belleville.

This is one of many empty farm homes found in the ghost farm community along the Mississagi River west of Blind River. The sandy stone-free soil seemed fertile at first, but after a few harvests, lost that fertility, forcing farm families to flee.

Abandoned and burnt out, this stone farm house stands on Neilson Ave. in northeastern Scarborough, surrounded by Toronto's relentlessly advancing urban fringe. Built in 1860 and owned for many years by the Neilson family, the house is being restored as part of a district park.

Many farms failed to advance beyond the pioneer phase on the rugged stony soils of St. Joseph Island in the St. Mary's River east of Sault Sainte Marie. This log cabin may have been the settlers' first home.

This settler's shanty sits abandoned near the shores of the Rainy River west of Fort Frances. A colonization road was built along the river linking the towns of Fort Frances and Rainy River. The rich black prairie-like soils spawned a prosperous farming community. Few original shanties or cabins lasted much beyond the very early years.

All alone in an overgrown meadow, this simple farm home lies near Thunder Bay. Despite these northerly latitudes, many areas around Thunder Bay contain pockets of relatively fertile soil, enough to have attracted large numbers of pioneer farmers.

A typical storey-and-a-half frame farm home stands empty. It is situated on St. Joseph Island, an island community near Sault Ste. Marie that still retains much of its pioneer flavour.

This two-storey house provided comfort for a farm family in the northern reaches of what was Frontenac County, an area where the fertility of the land was low, driving away many farmers.

A stone farm house near Perth is being mined for its building material, a fate common in a province where legal protection for heritage buildings is non-existent.

A log cabin near the eastern Ontario village of L'Amoureux is slowly being reclaimed by nature. The village, which lies between Ottawa and Hawkesbury, was founded by French-Canadian farmers. The place is now little more than a ghost town.

This simple home was one of the last to survive in an ex-slave settlement north of Shanty Bay. This area of Oro Township north of Barrie no longer contains descendants of the fugitive slaves who followed the Underground Railroad. However, an African church, built in the 1840s, still stands nearby and offers mute testimony to those difficult days.

Simcoe County's Gloucester Road was an early mail road which linked the villages of Mount St. Louis with Coldwater. It is now just an abandoned trail. This farm home was one of the few along it.

Most of the inhabitants were removed from Point Pelee National Park when it was created nearly 90 years ago. This home is now preserved by park authorities as a reminder of the park's early history.

Ontario's northern Clay Belt claimed many victims from among the novice farmers sent to settle it following the first world war. Flies and fierce winters sent most of them fleeing back south. One of their simple early cabins still stands near the town of Hearst.

With its rusting pump, this simple cabin stands vacant in the once-booming mining town of Wabigoon in northwestern Ontario. Now a residential community, Wabigoon was once the jumping-off point for prospectors heading south to seek their fortune in the Manitou Lakes' gold fields in the 1880s and 90s. The village lies near the Trans Canada Highway a short distance east of Dryden.

Frame Georgian style homes were once common among Ontario's earliest settled areas. This long-abandoned example stood in the Nanticoke area. It was unusual for such early dwellings not to be replaced by more substantial brick homes.

A log cabin north of Dryden is covered with clay, a rarely-used form of exterior treatment nowadays. It was the usual practice to chink the space between the logs with moss or mortar.

Pattern book farm homes were once the rage in rural Ontario, various designs being published in farm magazines during the 19th century. This L-shaped example stands abandoned near Lorneville.

Log cabins survive in only a few areas of Ontario, such as the Ottawa Valley, the Canadian Shield and parts of Victoria County. Because farms were less prosperous in these areas of low fertility farm families often did not replace the sturdy log cabins.

Sidings made of wood shingles have almost been universally replaced with aluminum siding. This rare survivor stood in Oxenden near Wiarton.

A rare surviving shanty, built by a Peter Robinson settler near Peterborough, lived out its last years as a chicken coop. Robinson was a noted colonizer who helped bring hundreds of Irish families to what is now the Peterborough area during the late 1820s. For an original settler's shanty to survive, even as an outbuilding, is unusual. Sadly there is no legal way in Ontario to protect such rare, historic structures.

Bridges

We drive over them and under them. We use them every day, but we rarely ever really see them. They are our heritage bridges. And they are fast disappearing.

From the earliest logs felled across a rampaging brook to the sleek concrete structures that today carry twelve lanes of congested traffic, bridges have been vital to getting us where we want to go. The first bridge to carry Europeans across Toronto's Don River was sketched by Lady Simcoe and was simply a log. Humble as it was, it carried York's first villagers from those twelve notoriously muddy blocks at the foot of today's Parliament St. to their first mills on the Don River, a site preserved today in Todmorden's historical park.

But the need to connect the fledgling capital with its pioneer hinterland meant building bridges that could carry a wagon or a stagecoach. These crude structures were at first just a row of logs laid crossways along more logs, and were both bone-jarring and dangerous. Logs often rotted quickly, leaving the hapless stage coach of travelers to lurch into a gap in the bridge, or worse, into the rocky gorge itself.

With no government agency in place dedicated to road maintenance (some might argue that little has changed), a law was passed which required settlers to perform 12 days labour each years on the repair and maintenance of the roads which served their lands. Little wonder that for years the voyage by stage between Toronto and Kingston took five days to complete.

As settlers opened up the land and performed their twelve days of road labour, bridges gradually improved. One of the first engineered bridge styles was known as the "King's truss" and consisted of two beams leaning against a central upright post. The longer "Queen's truss" style of bridge involved two uprights.

Finally, in 1840, concerned that the deplorable condition of the bridges left the colony indefensible, the British government allocated 1.5 million pounds (approximately $35 million in today's Canadian dollars) for bridge improvements. Over the following eight years, superintendent of roads, Casimir Gzowski, used the windfall to build 43 new bridges. Later Sir Casimir, he was also the great-grandfather of the well-known writer-broadcaster Peter Gzowski.

In 1849 a new Municipal Act downloaded the responsibility for bridges onto Ontario's newly legislated municipalities. But only a few years would pass before those municipalities became more interested in railways than in roads, and once more bridge construction languished. In fact, the railway bridges constructed during this period influenced the engineering techniques used on later road bridges.

Ironically, it was the railways themselves that brought the roads under increasing use, as farmers hauled more produce to the stations. With the heavier traffic, better bridges were desperately needed. The first big adaptation of railway technology to road bridges was the use of the wrought iron truss bridges. In the 1880s the much more durable steel replaced iron as the material of choice.

As the century drew to a close, reinforced concrete came into vogue, and has remained the main ingredient in bridge building to this day.

A number of bridge styles, common elsewhere, are rare in Ontario. Unlike in Quebec and the Maritimes, the covered bridge was not a tradition with the Royal Engineers who constructed many of Ontario's early bridges. Nor was there a sufficient supply of the wooden shingles necessary for the sides and roof. Similarly, Ontario saw few suspension bridges. Only three were constructed in Ontario, all in York county, and all by the same roads engineer, Frank Barber. Although not universal in Ontario, several swing bridges remain along the Rideau and Trent Canals, some still operated by hand as part of Parks Canada's policy of protecting the heritage of these historic waterways. Nor were stone bridges commonly built. Survivors include those at Lyndurst, St Mary's, Pakenham, and Smiths Falls. The oldest, that which spanned Webster's Falls, was demolished in the 1980s, in an era of supposed heritage enlightenment.

Despite the rapid disappearance, some bridges are gaining appreciation. The nine-arch, concrete bowstring bridge in Caledonia and the railway swing bridge to Little Current, the only road access to the world's largest freshwater island, are both community landmarks. The stone bridges at St. Mary's and Pakenham, as well as the covered bridge at West Montrose, have all been upgraded by the usually disinterested Ontario government. Nevertheless, needless losses continue. Despite lengthy and vocal public protest, the landmark bowstring bridge in Eden Mills was ripped from its location and reduced to rubble.

Today, more bridges are being protected, preserved and plaqued, and left as a legacy to the evolution of transportation in Ontario. Still, the perceived need for wider and faster roadways to hurry us to the next traffic jam continues to remove countless historic bridges all across Ontario.

The Lyndhurst stone arch bridge, now Ontario's oldest stone bridge, and one of the few built in the province, recalls the earliest days of concerted bridge building.

The West Montrose covered bridge was one of only five such bridges in Ontario (the others were at Napanee, Stirling, Frankford and Trenton). Located east of Elmira just south of Regional Road 86, it is the lone survivor. Here, the horses and buggies of the local Mennonite population often echo through the structure, giving it a genuine 19th century aura.

This iron truss bridge crosses Muskoka's Black River and is one of cottage country's lesser-known heritage features. As historical sites, bridges too often take a back seat to churches, mansions and mills.

The federal government has intentionally retained hand-operated swing bridges to help preserve the heritage of the ancient Rideau Canal. This bridge spans the Narrows lock between Upper and Lower Rideau lakes. Built between 1826 and 1832 as a military bypass to the more vulnerable St. Lawrence River, the Rideau Canal, with its massive stone dams and locks, was considered an engineering marvel in its days.

Sewell's bridge over the Rouge River in Toronto is the sole survivor of a trio of rare suspension bridges built in York County. The bridge lies within the Rouge River Provincial Park near the well-known Toronto Zoo.

One decidedly different way to celebrate the heritage of a bridge is demonstrated by the floral arrangements on this bridge which crosses the Beaver River south of Heathcote.

Train travelers once had to cross this wooden bridge to reach Coldwater's CN station. The depot is now a private house and the bridge is severed.

This small pony truss bridge likewise once led to the site of a railway station, that of the CPR at Britt, Ontario. Like that in Coldwater, the Britt station has been converted to a dwelling.

In southern Ontario wooden bridges are quickly vanishing and are being replaced with smoother concrete structures. This survivor carries Lakeshore Road across the CP tracks near Newcastle.

Thanks to a still plentiful (although dwindling) supply of lumber, wooden bridges are still being used in northern Ontario. While that at Sioux Narrows is celebrated as North America's longest single span wooden bridge, this more modest structure is found at Eagle River west of Thunder Bay.

Private bridges need not conform to the more stringent standards imposed on public bridges, as this Ear Falls area bridge demonstrates. It crosses the Snake River and leads to a private fish camp.

Railway bridges enjoy a heritage all their own. On old Finch Avenue in Scarborough, the abandoned abutments of the ill-fated Canadian Northern Railway are framed by the still-used CPR bridge. How long will it be before Ontario's notorious urban sprawl changes this roadscape?

It's unlikely that too many tall vehicles will be passing beneath this low railway bridge. It formerly carried a CNR spur line through the Town of Parry Sound. Today the right of way is a waterfront trail for hikers and cyclists.

Many railway swing bridges now carry cars such as those which lead to Parry Island near Parry Sound, and to Little Current. That at Glen Ross north of Trenton, however, has been laid to rest beside the water of the Trent Canal.

Where roads have been straightened or closed, relic bridges lie deteriorating and overgrown. This concrete bowstring bridge is in the Minden area.

Bypassed by the busy traffic of Highways 9 and 10 at Orangeville, this tiny concrete bridge sits in a marsh largely forgotten.

Near the town of Stirling, an old concrete bridge is preserved on a bypassed portion of road that was transferred to a private owner.

Near the semi-ghost town of Orchardville, a Highway 6 bypass has meant this elegant bowstring bridge was saved.

Ontario's greatest concentration of surviving concrete bowstring bridges lies in Wellington County between Guelph and Elora. This example is found near the community of Living Springs.

Concrete bowstring bridges are among the more aesthetically pleasing of Ontario's bridge styles. However, in some cases the concrete tie above the bridge limits vehicles to a certain height, and usually dooms the structure to replacement. This bridge is also in Wellington County, close to the previous example.

Popular around the turn of century, concrete bowstring bridges began to replace the earlier truss bridges. This structure is also located in the Living Springs area of Wellington County.

A bridge style more endangered than the bowstring is the older steel truss style of bridge. This one, at Young's Point over the Trent Canal, was built in 1873 and is the province's oldest combined iron and steel truss bridge.

This well-maintained steel truss bridge crosses the Mississagi River near Blind River and is one of the longest of its kind in Ontario.

Truss bridges are still part of southwestern Ontario's landscape. This slender bridge crosses the Grand River near the village of Conestogo in the heart of Mennonite country north of Waterloo.

An iron truss bridge, now nearly a century old, crosses the Thames River between the towns of Chatham and London. A number still survive along lesser-used back roads in this area. However, excessive land severances, with their resulting heavier traffic, are threatening their numbers.

Sawmills

Although they often shared rivers with grist and flour mills, sawmills occupied a decidedly different place in our history. As with the first grist mills, Ontario's first sawmills were government built. Later, grants of land were offered to encourage settlers to build more. Then, as demand grew, the financial incentive alone was enough to encourage entrepreneurs.

Sawmills, too, were less dependent upon water as a source of power. Many of the early operations were wind-powered while manpower, tedious though it was, was the source for others. Through the early years of the 19th century, water became the main source of power driving the up and down blades slowly through the long, rough logs.

Gang saws (more than one blade) and circular saws speeded up the process during the later years of the century, while steam, generated by burning sawdust or other waste, removed the need for water entirely.

Ownership differed too. In the south, where the sawmills shared rivers with the grist mills, individual owners ran them. But as the forest frontier receded northward, large lumber companies dominated. Here often the same company logged, owned their own railways and operated their own massive mills. Sometimes huge logging companies operated several mills, the Sheppards of Georgian Bay, and J.R Booth in Algonquin Park were but two of many.

The many mills which ringed the shores of Lakes Huron and Superior during the late 1800s were replaced during the 1900s by railside mills once railways opened the interior forests of the north country.

In most cases the lumber companies erected mill villages nearby where mill hands lived in simple cabins constructed of log, shingle, or plank. These villages gradually disappeared as the timber was depleted. Following the second world war, the wide-scale granting of the timber licences to the multi-national pulp companies brought to an end much of the north's sawmilling legacy. One by one the mills fell silent, and

Once again privately owned, the Bell Rock sawmill still cuts logs using the power of the Depot Creek, a tributary of the Napanee River. Built in 1920, new by most mill standards, it occupies the site of one of four mills that sawed lumber in the town. Most of that was for the Rathbun Lumber Company, which with its mills in Deseronto and its limits around the Depot Lakes, was once one of Ontario's largest lumber companies. Located north of Kingston, the Bell Rock mill was, for a number of years, operated by the conservation authority.

the villages disappeared. Two such villages persisted in southern Ontario into the early 1970s, one, in the Copeland Forest of Simcoe County, the other at Massanoga in Lennox and Addington County.

The remarkable and picturesque sawmill village at Tionaga near Foleyet stood intact until the 1980s when the owners of the adjacent fish camp removed the log cabins, cookhouse and burner. Although Ontario's Ministry of Citizenship and Culture, the government agency ostensibly responsible for the province's built heritage, was made aware of this outstanding village, they made no effort to save it.

Thanks to such indifference to Ontario's lumber and logging heritage, little remains to recall this vital chapter in our province's history. That makes the preservation efforts that do exist that much more outstanding. The O'Hara mill near Madoc has been preserved in a conservation area. The Hope mill, only a few miles distant, has similarly been saved, as has the Scott mill at Milford, and the Sovereen mill at Delhi.

Private preservation efforts are many and include the water-powered Bell Rock mill north of Napanee, which uses the water of the river to cut logs for local farmers, and the Haines mill at Cheltenham, now a private home. The rambling sawmill at Balaclava, which used the water from Constan Creek to cut logs for nearly a century, until it ceased operation in the late 1960s, awaits a badly needed saviour.

These however, are the exceptions. By the end of the 20th century most sawmills and their villages had vanished.

How much longer will the Balaclava mill last? Following its closing in the late 1960s, this water-powered sawmill has failed to find a new owner who might somehow preserve this Renfrew County landmark. The mill has stood since the 1860s. The community was settled in the 1830s by squatters and until the post office opened was known as Brunswick Bush. Now a ghost town, Balaclava also contains a general store and blacksmith shop, both abandoned, and until recently, the former hotel. It, however, burned, a fate which may well befall the mill unless this historic prize is somehow saved.

A feature of Ontario's logging industry was the log flume, used to drive logs around such obstacles as rapids and waterfalls. This rare survivor stands beside the thundering falls on the Pigeon River which forms Canada's international boundary southwest of Thunder Bay.

Recently burned, the massive mill at Field was the community's main industry. With its computer-operated saws, the mill attracted visitors to see this historic landmark. Today the town has nothing. Field is an otherwise inauspicious little hamlet located northwest of North Bay.

The picturesque Hurdville mill once stood in the district of Parry Sound. Neither its visual appeal nor its history could save the doomed structure. The mill was located on the Manitouwabing River, a few kilometers east of the town of Parry Sound. The community was reported to have had a population of 500 in 1885. Today it has fewer than 50.

By the mid-1970s the mill at Massanoga was in ruin, although much of the mill village stood intact. Little other than rubble marks the site today. Relatively recent by historical standards, the Massanoga mill was built in 1938 by the Sawyer-Stoll lumber company. The little town could boast three bunkhouses, a dozen cabins and a recreation hall, all company

Despite being one of northern Ontario's best examples of a sawmill town, these cabins, along with the log cookhouse and sawmill burner, located on the shore of Horwood Lake near Foleyet, were removed. The sawmill was operated by the Pineland Lumber Company, one of several, until the company shut down the mill in 1957 and moved the operation

One of the prettiest villages along Lake Superior's north shore is the historic community of Rossport. Along with the CP Railway and fishing, the sawmill represented an important economic link in the life of the community. Today the trains roar right through, and the derelict mill has vanished.

The O'Hara mill, near Madoc, has been preserved in a conservation area. It may have been built as early as 1837, and was operated by Squire James O'Hara and his descendants from 1847 until 1908. A muley operation, the technique involved two upright bales, powered by the flow of the water, which cut on the down stroke, a far slower operation than the hand-powered saws more common at that time. The mill was purchased by the Moira River Conservation Authority in 1954, and resumed operation as a living museum in 1957. Today the Ontario government discourages conservation authorities from such "costly" heritage preservation.

The last cabin in the last of southern Ontario's sawmill villages was that at Copeland. The operation began in 1906 with the opening of a sawmill by Jasper Martin. In 1922 Charles Copeland expanded the business, adding a larger mill, and a townsite with a store, school and several wood shingle cabins. The mill burned in 1959 and was replaced with a smaller structure, until it also ceased operation in 1974. Once a landmark to motorists traveling the adjacent Highway 400 Extension north of Barrie, the entire village was removed by the Ministry of Natural Resources.

Country roads

One could legitimately ask, "Whatever happened to country driving?" We all remember those sunny summer Sundays when Mom would make ham sandwiches and Dad would hustle everyone into the car for a drive in the country. We would follow those shady lanes, pausing to watch a tractor grumble slowly through a field of rich chocolate-coloured dirt. Pulling onto the shoulder we would unfold the blanket, unwrap the sandwiches from the waxed paper and quarrel over who was getting the larger portion of Coke. Then, somewhere in the distance, a lonely train whistle would announce a crossing, while the column of smoke from its steam engine would glide above a distant row of trees.

Sadly, those days are gone. Four lane roads now slice across the country, taking with them the twists and turns and the shady rows of maples. Excessive land severances have turned the pastoral landscape into one of rural sprawl. Trucks roar by almost incessantly. Country roads have become just another feature disappearing from Ontario's country horizons.

In the beginning, roads, where they existed at all, were scarcely passable muddy lanes beset by broken bridges, windfalls, and jolting potholes. A few trails followed Indian paths, like the Hockley Road. Later, settlement roads punctured the dark forests like the Kingston Road, its predecessor the Danforth Road, the Talbot Road, and the roads to the Owen Sound area, like the Garafraxa Road and the Sydenham Road.

Then came the surveyors. To make order of the wilderness, they divided the province up into townships, most being approximately ten miles square. These were in turn surveyed into farm lots, with concession roads crossing the front of each. To allow farmers to pass from one concession road to the next, side roads were surveyed at intervals of every five to ten lots.

Surveyors were frequently criticized for having a less than steady eye. They worked "without a compass or pickets, but with grog and confusion," noted one critic. Because not every township enjoyed identical configuration, concession roads

Many of the scenic roads that mount the Niagara Escarpment were published in an early version of the Niagara Escarpment plan only to be removed at the request of local politicians who didn't want "city people" wearing out their roads. A few have since become marked as scenic routes.

seldom met up at township boundaries. Diversions and doglegs were the norm at such junctures. Where roads met at sharp angles, the parcels within the wedge were known as gores. One former township indeed went by the name "Toronto Gore Township." Otherwise, Ontario's country roads were as straight as the topography would permit. Neither lake nor mountain could divert a British army surveyor from laying out a straight road, or at least trying to.

Once the forests were cleared, winter winds swept across the open fields blasting the snow from the roads, making travel difficult for sleighs. To remedy this problem, many municipalities paid farmers up to 25 cents a tree to plant windbreaks along the roads. Because winter travel was faster in snow, this was more to keep the snow from blowing off the roads, than from being blown onto it.

There arrived, however, a time when automobiles and horse drawn vehicles vied for the same road space. While the teamsters preferred the snow to be left on the ground in the winter, car drivers wanted it removed. For a time politicians compromised by clearing some roads and not others. Today, however, rural politicians are likely to receive a harsh early morning phone call if someone's road is not ploughed in time to head off for work.

Few of those shady lines of trees remain, as the dictates of the auto age meant wider roads, and longer site lines. Age, too, has taken its toll, as many of those trees have reached maturity and must be cut. A few communities are replanting, but sadly these are a minority and now much of Ontario's country roadscapes have become barren and treeless.

Another feature of Ontario's country roads were the fences. During the early years of clearing, rubble was simply piled up along the roads to prevent animals from wandering. But once the trees were gone, farmers were anxious to demarcate both the fields and property lines, using whatever material was close at hand. Stumps of rot-resistant pine were yanked from the sandy soils and placed along the roads in the Norfolk and Rice Lake areas especially. Log fences were common in eastern Ontario, while cedar rail fences tended to be more commonplace on the Canadian shield and in southwestern Ontario.

Stone fences were less common in Ontario. They were not moveable, a feature many farmers found desirable, and required construction skills few farmers possessed. However, in areas of Ontario where stone workers were found, such as in Wellington County and parts of northern Halton, stone fences can still be seen. English style hedgerows and plank fences, however, never caught on.

The fate of the Ontario fence line has varied. In the 1860s wire fences were introduced, and in many areas they soon replaced the old wooden fence lines. In parts of the Greater Toronto Area, where hobby farming has replaced the real thing, many cedar or log fences have been resurrected for their aesthetic appeal. In areas of marginal farming such as the Bruce Peninsula or the Canadian Shield, log fences lie overgrown, a symbol of the hardship and broken dreams that befell hopeful pioneer settlers in these harsh lands. But throughout Ontario, the ever-present road wideners have taken their toll all in the name of the auto. Farm modernization, too, has seen fields widened and fences removed or replaced with the more recent electrical fence.

All have taken their toll on the country road. Road widening, tree removal, and new fences have altered the rural landscape and made the country road a thing of the past.

The view from Mount Wolfe in the Albion Hills is now besmirched by monster homes and a wide paved road. The Albion Hills represent a portion of the Oak Ridges Moraine, a picturesque and environmentally sensitive ridge of sand and gravel left by melting glaciers 20,000 years ago. Conflicts frequently arise over the best use of the scenic hills, usually setting gravel owners against home owners against recreation proponents.

An unusual style of cedar rail fence is located in Lanark County in eastern Ontario. Their light weight, straightness, and durability made cedar rail the most popular fencing material among early farmers.

A cedar rail fence in Halton Region demonstrates the more typical zig-zag pattern. Despite the advent of barbed wire in the 1850s, and electric fencing a century later, cedar rail fences still abound.

Ontario's earliest roads were constructed of logs, especially where the route was low lying. They were known as "corduroy" because of their resemblance to that material. This rare surviving section of corduroy road is found in Awenda Provincial Park.

Cedar rail fences still enfold the fields at the foot of Skinners Bluff near Wiarton. Many land owners have retained their cedar fencing as much for its aesthetic appeal as for its longevity.

This rare relic road, now a farm field, was once lined with birch trees and fences of pine stumps. Where they could be easily extracted from sandy soils, pine stumps made for durable fences. This view is near Uxbridge.

Stone fences were less common in Ontario than were those of cedar rail as rails could be moved more easily. This stone fence is located near Blair just south of Kitchener. With their knowledge of stone-work, many Scottish settlers preferred stone fences.

Dairy farms dot the idyllic country landscape on a crisp fall day near Thunder Bay.

The Beaver Valley still contains a few attractive country roads. Here a section of cedar fence lines the road between Heathcote and Kimberley.

To open the wilderness of the Ottawa Huron tract to settlement, and to facilitate large scale logging, the government opened a series of colonization roads. The land was free, but the poor soils forced the disheartened settlers out soon after the logging companies had cleared the forests. These early trails are today both scenic and historic corridors. Here the Addington Colonization Road mounts the rocky hills near Quadeville, a village located east of Bancroft.

Algoma country, north of Sault Ste. Marie, contains roads that wind through a landscape of lofty hills and pastoral valleys. This scene unfolds near the ghost town of Havilah.

A rare example of a tree lined road, this one has withstood the chain saws of the road wideners and still survives near Erin.

This winding Dufferin County road has now been straightened and this pretty hillock removed. The need for straighter roads and better sight lines has cost Ontario many of its once scenic routes.

Danforth Road, the first to link York (now Toronto) with eastern Ontario was too winding and was soon replaced with the straighter Kingston Road. This small section of the Danforth Road lies near Cobourg. Another is found near Grafton.

Natural obstacles did not deter the early road surveyors from laying out roads in uncompromising straight lines. This view is near Osler Bluff south of Collingwood.

A once vital farm side road south of Rice Lake is now an unmaintained seasonal road. Many early farm roads laid out by 19th century surveyors are no longer used, as farms have been abandoned or amalgamated. Where they haven't been sold to adjacent land owners, such tracks are now suitable only for hiking or for snowmobiles.

This former farm road north of Rice Lake is now a private lane. Like many in Ontario, it was sold to an adjacent owner when it was no longer needed as a through route.

Mines

Nothing is perhaps more haunting, or more symbolic of disappearing Ontario, than a skeletal headframe. Rising above the harsh bare rock or a scraggly young forest, they bespeak the short-lived nature of the province's resource wealth. But unlike timber, a mineral deposit cannot regenerate itself. Once the mineral is gone, there is no regeneration, and the headframe is the headstone of that vanished treasure.

Mining in Ontario was a native pastime long before starry-eyed prospectors began to scour the hills. The Ojibway and the Ottawa Indians would pry the soft copper from the rocky shores of Lakes Superior and Huron to craft into trade items. It should be no surprise then that Ontario's earliest non-native mining was of those very copper deposits. But the copper often meant that other minerals were present as well, and the search soon switched to one for gold and silver. The massive silver deposit at Silver Islet, now a ghost town on the north shore of Lake Superior, began as a search for copper. And the copper legacy of Sudbury, the world's nickel capital, survives to this day in the name of the community that headquarters the mine, Copper Cliff.

While the names most commonly associated with Ontario's golden legacy are Porcupine, Kirkland Lake, Red Lake and Geraldton, Ontario's first gold rush took place far to the south, just a few miles from the north shore of Lake Ontario. Here, near today's Madoc, prospector Marcus Powell literally stumbled into what many thought to be a valley of gold. Towns with golden names like Eldorado, Deloro, and Cordova soon became boom towns. But the deposits proved either too small, too difficult to process, or just plain fraudulent. The mines were short-lived and most of the towns became gaunt reminders of their heyday. Meanwhile, the site of the first golden lode lies neglected in the forest mere metres from a busy highway, its whereabouts known to only a few.

Later, as the rails were laid across the difficult terrain of northern Ontario, prospectors followed, hopping off the

The mills and headframes of the ghost town of Gold Rock have been silent for nearly a century, yet they still hold on in the woods near Dryden. The town was once the hub of activity for a half dozen gold mines clustered on the shores of the Manitou Lakes. This view depicts the Laurentian mill.

trains to explore any signs of glittering wealth. They weren't disappointed. Soon golden boom towns like Kirkland Lake, Porcupine, Red Lake and Gold Rock were household names. Cobalt, Silver Islet and Silver Centre were the result of the silver rushes, while Sudbury and its collection of mining towns became the world's leading nickel producer.

While mining remains a leading employer in Ontario's north country, many of the boom towns have become much quieter, a few becoming ghost towns. Silver Centre, near Cobalt and once home to 700, has reverted to bush. The headframes and stamping mills of Gold Rock rise above the remote woods south of Dryden, while waves now wash unimpeded over the Silver Islet shoal in Lake Superior, a rock that could once boast Canada's richest silver mine. And while Cobalt is slowly coming back to life as a tourist destination, two dozen headframes of its silver mines dot the scrubby rocks around the town.

The Deloro mill was one of the mines that gave rise to the raucous miners' village of Gold Rock. Although the mines reached their peak of operation around the turn of the century, some were operated off and on up until the 1930s.

Kirkland Lake, where the streets were once literally lined with gold, owes its existence to the legendary Harry Oates, whose mansion still stands, now a museum. This skeletal headframe, however, more fittingly bespeaks the fate of the goldfield.

Near Red Lake, the MacKenzie Island gold mine has been silent for many years now. Although the townsite is nearly a ghost town, several families still call the island home.

This Cobalt silver mine headframe rises above the landscape, as do two dozen other headframcs around this once booming mining town where the population surpassed 10,000. Today the town is less than a third that size, and the headframes are silent.

Kerr Lake, near Cobalt, was drained to allow the bottom to be worked. The waters have returned, reflecting the remains of the headframe.

One of Cobalt's more modest headframes still stands guard over a small grove of trees. An annotated self-guiding map, available at the mining museum in Cobalt, leads to a discovery of the ruins of many of the area's abandoned mines.

More typical of southern Ontario's mining legacy are the ruins of the Cheltenham brick works, closed for four decades, and now preserved for their heritage. Timothy Findley's book, THE WARS, was made into a movie on this site.

One of the few gold mines worked in southern Ontario was the Ore Chimney mine in eastern Ontario. Despite its brief life, the mine has left extensive ruins, although this headframe is now gone. The mine was located north of Kaladar which lies on Highway 7 east of Peterborough.

Typically, the townsite of Cobalt is guarded by headframes at its eastern and western approaches. Tunnels and shafts beneath the town have on occasion collapsed. One such "pothole" on Highway 11A, the main access to the town, cost several million dollars to repair.

Near Red Lake, the golden town of Madsen was a leading producer. These company buildings, however, became ghosts of the glory days. Several of the original gold deposits in the Red Lake region are now being re-prospected, and some have even resumed operation.

This monument lies near the spot where blacksmith Fred Larose threw a pick at a fox, thus revealing the deposit which became the Larose Mine. Despite local legend, the Larose strike was not Cobalt's first. That honour goes to McKinley and Darraugh, two timber scouts who literally stumbled upon the worlds' richest silver bearing rocks.

Stamping mills and refineries were as much a part of the mining landscape as were the headframes. This former plant lies near Cobalt.

A rickety bridge led to the north-western Ontario gold mine of Olive. Nearby are the ghost towns of Mine Centre, Chief City, Seine City and Turtle City. Despite the aspirations evident in their names, only Mine Centre grew to any size. All have long vanished.

The Geraldton gold rush of the 1920s and 30s spawned a forest of headframes. Many, however, are now removed, and a piece of Ontario's mining legacy has gone with them. Small townsites huddled at their feet where a few residents still live.

Ignored by many, and unknown to most, the ruins of Ontario's first gold mine lie hidden in a Hastings County forest. Prospector Bob Bredberg, shown here, hopes to change all that by making the site available to all Ontarians. The site lies within paces of Highway 62 a short distance north of Madoc.

Barns

Ontario's best known country icon, found everywhere, is the barn. Little else typifies Ontario's rural landscape better than this ubiquitous structure. They have played a role that was vital and fundamental to the rural economy and landscape. Yet they, too, are vanishing. As farming changes from the family farm to agri-business, many are replaced by more modern agricultural structures. Others are simply left to rot in idle and overgrown fields.

Ontario's first barns were crude log huts quickly piled together to house a few chickens and crops. As the pioneers cleared away the forests, larger areas could be put into crop or pasture. Mills appeared beside rushing streams and gave the farmers a market for their wheat. Larger barns were soon needed. Many were three or five bay barns with separate spaces for animals, feed and for winnowing. As prosperity increased frame barns replaced those made from logs.

During the closing years of the 19th century an agricultural revolution swept Ontario. Canada's western prairies were thrown open to settlers and the west replaced Ontario as Canada's wheat producer. Meanwhile, the dairy industry moved in to fill Ontario's farming void. Dairy herds needed new barns. Older barns were jacked up and put on foundations which contained the cattle stalls. Silos became a standard adjunct, being located at first inside the barn. Disgusted consumers soon discovered that the cattle feed and, thus, the milk, was picking up the barn smells and silos were quickly relegated to the outside.

But the joy in celebrating the heritage of Ontario's vanishing barns lies not in their sameness but in their differences. Some of those differences reflect the age of the barns. A few of Ontario's surviving barns were built by the United Empire Loyalists and other settlers near the close of the 18th century. A few early board and batten structures, some with elegant cupolas, still stand in the Quinte area. In other areas, the original pioneer barns linger. Most of these, however, are found where the soil or the geography defeated most efforts to farm

profitably. The back roads of Haliburton, northern Hastings, Parry Sound and Muskoka contain these hardy survivors, many engulfed by overgrown meadows, others flanked by new country homes.

Other differences in barn styles reflect the ethnic origin of the settlers. Midwestern Ontario, for example, is home to the sturdy and massive Dutch barns, a style brought to Ontario by the savvy Mennonite and Pennsylvania Dutch immigrants and refugees. These remain the centrepiece of many a Mennonite farm to this day. The distinctive round-roofed barns of the Finns are found around Sudbury and in the mountains west of Thunder Bay. A concentration of solid stone barns sets Wellington County aside as the heartland of Ontario's Scottish settlers. The banks of the Ottawa River and the rugged Northern Clay belt attracted French Canadians with their long, low and often colourful barns.

The Ottawa Valley, perhaps Ontario's most distinctive cultural region, has a barn style uniquely its own—the string barn. Here the original barn was added to as farms prospered. Hence they have taken on the appearance of a string of barns connected together, some log, some frame.

Sadly, these differences are disappearing. Modernization, abandonments, and excessive land severance activity are all combining to eradicate the Ontario barn, the most loved and comforting of the country icons, from the landscapes they have called home for nearly two centuries.

A low, brightly painted barn in the Lac Ste.Therese area of Ontario's northern Clay Belt bespeaks its French origin. Many migrants to this area followed the rails of the Transcontinental Railway which originated in Quebec City. As a result, most of the villages and farms between Cochrane and Hearst were French Canadian.

Finnish settlers brought to many regions of northern Ontario their own distinctive barn styles with round roofs and a protrusion from the gable. They were attracted by the cheap land and the similarity of the terrain to that in their homeland.

Pioneer log barns still survive in this field on St. Joseph Island near Sault Ste. Marie. The rugged land and relative isolation of the island kept farmers from improving upon their operations, and many pioneer buildings linger on the St. Joseph landscape.

This log barn is in the village of Franktown in the Ottawa Valley. Located on the military road between Perth and Richmond, Franktown was laid out as a large townsite during the war of 1812. It failed to grow, and many of the surveyed streets and town lots have remained as empty fields.

A rare eight-sided farm building on Manitoulin Island. Eight-sided buildings, a style started in New York state, moved into Ontario during the 1840s and 50s. By 1900, Ontario could count more than 100 buildings, houses and barns alike, which incorporated this strange style.

A Finnish barn stands in isolation in a field west of Thunder Bay. Optimistic immigrants to Ontario's northwestern farmlands soon filled the fertile lands and spread into territory with lands less suitable for farming.

The harsh soils of northern Frontenac County defeated many efforts to farm profitably, leaving many farms in the pioneer stages. These structures are located near Sharbot Lake.

Recent owners have added a residence to this barn located west of Thunder Bay.

Log rooves are seldom found anymore on Ontario's farm structures. These logs have started to sprout a lawn of their own. This small stable is in Pass Lake, an area of good farmland east of Thunder Bay which was settled by Danish colonizers during the 1920s and '30s.

Even the stoutest of Wellington County's solid stone barns are subject to salvaging. The proliferation of such barns reflects the Scottish heritage of this region of Ontario.

The elegance of the Loyalist barn with its cupola and board and batten construction is occasionally still seen in the Quinte region of Ontario's Loyalist heartland.

A trio of abandoned barns catch the glow of evening sun on a Manitoulin Island hillside. Manitoulin is the world's largest freshwater island. Its relative inaccessibility has spared it the urban sprawl engulfing much of rural Ontario, and the associated unsightly intrusions into the landscape.

Even the remote mountains of Algoma attracted farm settlers, only to defeat them with stony soils and harsh winters. This scene is in the area of Searchmont, a station stop on the Algoma Central Railway.

The Ottawa Valley's distinctive string barn style is clearly demonstrated in this grouping located near Eganville. String barns evolved when farmers, rather than replacing early barns, simply added to them.

These Parry Sound hay barns were still in use in recent years. Their days are now numbered. Most of the land in the Parry Sound area proved suitable only for pasture and hay, and some could not provide even that.

The ghost farm settlement of Newfoundout contains a stunning collection of abandoned log barns. More than a dozen vacant farmsteads sit atop the Black Donald Mountains far from the nearest town, which in this case is Renfrew.

While the remains of iron wind pumps are still relatively plentiful, those constructed of wood are very rare. This example stands near the village of Magnetawan.

Wooden silos have been almost universally replaced by those made of aluminum or concrete. This rare survivor stands outside the town of Beaverton.

Another wooden silo, minus barn, stands in a field near Snow Road Ontario. Snow Road, named for an early surveyor, is a picturesque village located in the rolling hills of the Canadian Shield north of Kingston.

This Loyalist barn near Housic in eastern Ontario is surrounded by advancing bush.

The sad story of Ontario's "roads of broken dreams," the colonization roads which held out so much hope for settlers, but which ended in heartbreak, is reflected in this tumble-down barn on the Nipissing Road in Parry Sound.

The architectural craze which brought eight-sided houses to Ontario, also brought eight-sided barns. This barn, which once stood near Finch Avenue in Toronto, was moved to Ontario's agricultural museum near Milton.

These log barns served the Ferguson Stopping Place opened by John Ferguson in 1876 on the Mattawa Colonization Road near Deep River. Preserved for many years by Atomic Energy of Canada, the former hotel is now a bed and breakfast.

Index